AUG   2016

D1451068

THE BIG DIPPER

Joseph Stanley

PowerKiDS
press

New York

Published in 2016 by The Rosen Publishing Group, Inc.
29 East 21st Street, New York, NY 10010

Copyright © 2016 by The Rosen Publishing Group, Inc.

All rights reserved. No part of this book may be reproduced in any form without permission in writing from the publisher, except by a reviewer.

First Edition

Editor: Katie Kawa
Book Design: Katelyn Heinle

Photo Credits: Cover Yganko/Shutterstock.com; back cover, p. 1 nienora/Shutterstock.com; pp. 5, 16, 21 angelinast/Shutterstock.com; p. 7 Santia/Shutterstock.com; p. 9 lynea/Shutterstock.com; p. 10 Igor Kovalchuk/Shutterstock.com; p. 11 tomoki1970/Shutterstock.com; p. 13 Yuriy Kulik/Shutterstock.com; p. 15 AlexanderZam/Shutterstock.com; p. 17 Zurijeta/Shutterstock.com; p. 19 behindlens/Shutterstock.com; p. 22 Stuart O'Sullivan/The Image Bank/Getty Images.

Library of Congress Cataloging-in-Publication Data

Stanley, Joseph, author.
The Big Dipper / Joseph Stanley.
     pages cm. — (The constellation collection)
Includes bibliographical references and index.
ISBN 978-1-4994-0937-6 (pbk.)
ISBN 978-1-4994-0960-4 (6 pack)
ISBN 978-1-4994-1002-0 (library binding)
1. Ursa Major—Juvenile literature. 2. Constellations—Juvenile literature. 3. Constellations—Folklore—Juvenile literature. I. Title.
QB802.S73 2016
523.8—dc23
                          2015013037

Manufactured in the United States of America

CPSIA Compliance Information: Batch #WS15PK: For Further Information contact Rosen Publishing, New York, New York at 1-800-237-9932

CONTENTS

BIG DIPPER, BIG BEAR

On a clear night, the stars in the sky can sometimes look like giant connect-the-dots drawings. There are 88 groups of stars that form the shapes of people, animals, or objects and have been given a name based on their shape. These are constellations. Many smaller groups of stars also form certain shapes. These smaller groups of stars are called asterisms.

Many asterisms are found within larger constellations. The Big Dipper is one of the most famous asterisms because it's so easily seen. It's found within the constellation Ursa Major, or the Great Bear.

STAR STORY
The Big Dipper got its name from the fact that it looks like a big spoon with a long handle that people might use for dipping into drinking water.

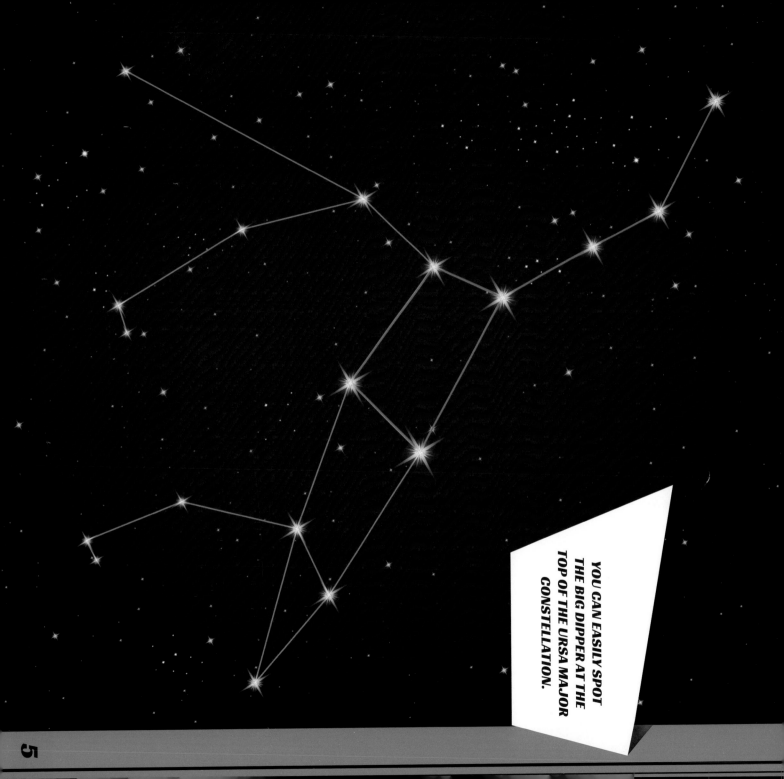

YOU CAN EASILY SPOT THE BIG DIPPER AT THE TOP OF THE URSA MAJOR CONSTELLATION.

MANY DIFFERENT NAMES

Astronomers are people who study the **planets**, stars, and other bodies in space. They've been doing this for centuries. Although certain astronomers are given credit for discovering planets, moons, and other space objects, it's impossible to say who discovered each constellation or asterism.

People from different **cultures** looked up at these star formations and saw different things. As such, constellations and asterisms had different names in different cultures. For example, the Big Dipper was seen as a plow pulled by oxen in some cultures. In India, it was said to be a group of wise men.

STAR STORY
In some cultures, the Big Dipper was seen as a wagon.

THE BIG DIPPER IS MADE UP OF SEVEN STARS, SO INDIAN ASTRONOMERS CALLED THE ASTERISM THE SEVEN SAGES. A SAGE IS A WISE PERSON.

A GREEK MYTH

The ancient Greeks created a **myth** to explain how a bear came to be placed among the stars. Zeus, who was the king of the Greek gods, fell in love with a **nymph** named Callisto. Zeus' wife, Hera, then changed Callisto into a bear because she was angry Zeus loved another woman.

Hunters chased Callisto, and even her own son, Arcas, tried to kill her. However, Zeus sent Callisto into the stars to save her. As he threw the bear into the sky, its tail was **stretched**. This is why Ursa Major has such a long tail of stars, which is the handle of the Big Dipper.

STAR STORY

The ancient Greek myth of Callisto stated that Zeus turned Arcas into a bear before he could kill his mother. Zeus also sent Arcas into the sky. This smaller bear is known as the constellation Ursa Minor.

URSA MAJOR IS ONE OF MANY CONSTELLATIONS WHOSE NAME CAN BE TRACED BACK TO AN ANCIENT GREEK MYTH.

NATIVE AMERICAN STORIES

The ancient Greeks weren't the only people to look into the sky and see a bear. Many Native American tribes also told stories to explain how a bear ended up in the stars. While they did see the same bear shape in Ursa Major, there was one big difference—the bear they saw didn't have a tail.

STAR STORY

Ursa Major is low in the sky in the Northern Hemisphere during fall. This is why Native Americans connected the story of Ursa Major to the changing color of the leaves in the fall.

Instead of a tail, the Native Americans saw the three stars that make up the Big Dipper's handle as hunters. When the hunters shot the bear with their arrows, its blood made the leaves turn red in the fall.

NATIVE AMERICAN TRIBES USED ONE MYTH TO EXPLAIN BOTH THE URSA MAJOR CONSTELLATION AND THE REASON LEAVES TURN RED IN THE FALL.

NAMING THE STARS

The seven stars that make up the Big Dipper have names that come from the Arabic language. Arabic was the language of the Middle Eastern astronomers who studied many constellations and asterisms.

Merak and Dubhe are the two stars that make up the edge of the Big Dipper's bowl that's farthest from the handle. "Merak" means "the **loins**" of the Great Bear in Arabic. "Dubhe" comes from an Arabic phrase that refers to the star's place on the back of the Great Bear. These two stars are also called pointer stars. They point the way to Polaris, or the North Star.

STAR STORY

Dubhe is the second-brightest star in the Big Dipper. The brightest is Alioth, which is the third star from the end of the handle.

ALIOTH

MERAK

DUBHE

MERAK, DUBHE, AND ALIOTH ARE THREE IMPORTANT STARS IN THE BIG DIPPER.

POINTING TO POLARIS

Merak and Dubhe's role as pointer stars is important because they're pointing to one of the most important stars in the sky. Polaris is the brightest star in the sky that appears over the North Pole. If you drew an imaginary line down from Polaris, it would run almost perfectly through the North Pole.

Polaris has helped people navigate, or find their way, for centuries. If you move toward Polaris, you will always know you're traveling north. During the time of slavery in the United States, slaves escaped to freedom in northern states by following Polaris.

STAR STORY

If you move toward Polaris, you're moving northward. South is behind you. East is to your right. West is to your left.

POLARIS IS PART OF AN ASTERISM CALLED THE LITTLE DIPPER. THIS ASTERISM IS PART OF THE URSA MINOR CONSTELLATION, WHICH IS ALSO KNOWN AS THE LITTLE BEAR.

POLARIS ←

THE HORSE AND RIDER

Mizar, which is another of the stars in the Big Dipper, isn't actually one star—it's made up of a pair of binary stars. A binary star is a pair of stars that orbit, or spin, around a shared center. This makes Mizar a **quadruple** star system, or a group of four stars.

Mizar is very close to a star just outside the Big Dipper that's named Alcor. Alcor is also a binary star. Astronomers from the Middle East used to call Mizar and Alcor the "Horse and Rider" because they were so close.

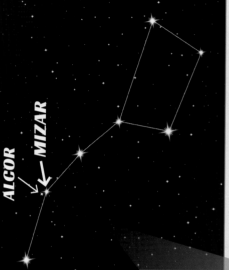

ALCOR

MIZAR

STAR STORY

The name "Mizar" comes from the Arabic word for a veil or **cloak.** "Alcor" comes from an Arabic word that means "the faint one."

PEOPLE FROM DIFFERENT CULTURES BELIEVED IT WAS A SIGN OF GOOD EYESIGHT IF SOMEONE COULD SEE BOTH MIZAR AND ALCOR IN THE SKY INSTEAD OF SEEING THEM AS ONE STAR.

AN EYE ON THE HORIZON

Some constellations and asterisms are only **visible** in the sky at certain times of the year. However, if you live in the Northern Hemisphere, you should be able to find the Big Dipper at any time of the year. The Big Dipper never disappears below the horizon, which is what happens to some other star formations. The horizon is the line where the sky meets the ground or water.

While the Big Dipper never disappears below the horizon, it does look different during each season. It changes its position in the sky around Polaris.

STAR STORY

It's hardest to see the Big Dipper in the fall, because that's the season when the asterism is closest to the horizon.

THE HORIZON IS THE LINE THE SUN SEEMS TO DISAPPEAR UNDER AT SUNSET AND REAPPEAR FROM AT SUNRISE.

CHANGING POSITIONS

It's easy to understand the way the Big Dipper changes position during the seasons if you think about it as a circle. Polaris is always at the center of the circle.

If you look at Polaris in the spring, the Big Dipper is above it and flipped upside down, with its bowl facing west. In the summer, the Big Dipper is to the left of Polaris, with the bowl pointing down. If you face north in the fall, it's below Polaris. Finally, in the winter, it's to the right of Polaris and has its bowl pointing up.

STAR STORY

For centuries, astronomers have used star charts to study the sky. Star charts are maps of the night sky that point out stars, constellations, and other important bodies in space.

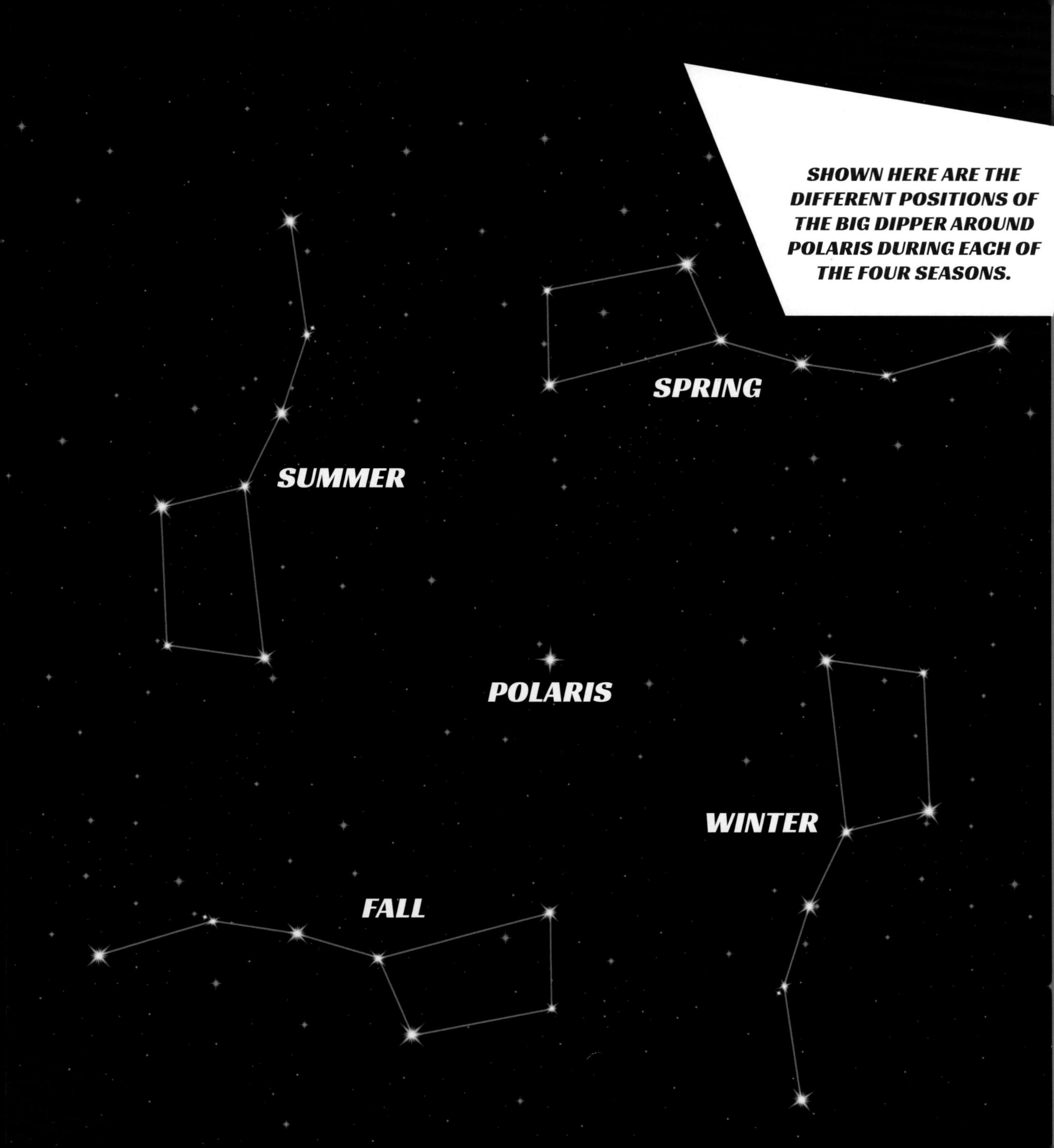

FALL

SUMMER

POLARIS

SPRING

WINTER

SHOWN HERE ARE THE DIFFERENT POSITIONS OF THE BIG DIPPER AROUND POLARIS DURING EACH OF THE FOUR SEASONS.

CAN YOU FIND IT?

The Big Dipper is one of the most common star formations people look for in the night sky. Its simple shape and bright stars make it easy for even beginning stargazers to spot with just their eyes. The easiest way to find the Big Dipper and other star formations is to go outside on a clear night in an area away from man-made light. Be sure to have an adult with you.

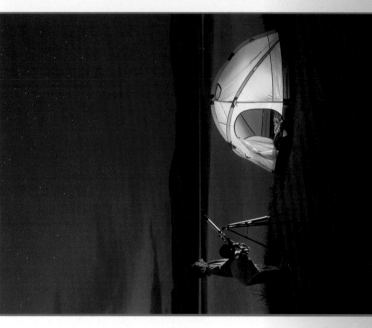

Once you find the Big Dipper, see if you can spot the rest of the Ursa Major constellation. You can even find the North Star!

GLOSSARY

cloak: A loose outer piece of clothing that is like a coat.

culture: The beliefs and ways of life of a certain group of people.

hemisphere: Half of Earth.

loin: An area on the back and sides of an animal's body near the tail.

myth: A story told in ancient cultures to explain a practice, belief, or part of nature.

nymph: A spirit in the shape of a young woman.

planet: A large, round object in space that travels around a star.

quadruple: Made up of four parts.

stretched: Pulled tightly.

visible: Able to be seen.

INDEX

WEBSITES

Due to the changing nature of Internet links, PowerKids Press has developed an online list of websites related to the subject of this book. This site is updated regularly. Please use this link to access the list: www.powerkidslinks.com/tcc/tbd